# Acting on Fire

## Acting Exercises for One Person
## Without a Scene Partner

# Julie Ann Fay

# DEDICATION

I dedicate this to my mother, Ruta Fay, a single mom and incredible lady. She always believes in my dreams even when she doesn't always understand them. I cherish you more than you know!

# ACKNOWLEDGMENTS

To all the great actors out there who spend tireless hours reading books, observing performances and doing their own exercises with and without scene partners, I thank you for being the inspiration for this book.

# CONTENTS

# CONTENTS SORTED BY ACTING SKILLS

# HOW TO USE THIS BOOK

This book can be used in multiple ways. Originally it was created as a series of exercises to be done in order one through 60 with a bonus page of techniques to help an actor cry on command.

Because of that, I shuffled around various aspects of the actor's craft instead of lumping each aspect together and doing an entire chapter on auditioning followed by an entire chapter on character etc. I know when I'm practicing something like acting that involves so many creative aspects within it, I want a little variety while I practice. Acting is at its best when it's spontaneous and often unpredictably exciting. The closest I could get to replicate this in book form was to shuffle the acting techniques instead of pooling them together.

However, if you prefer to work on one type of acting technique at a time I have included a second set of contents where each acting exercise's page is listed alongside its matching acting skill.

The exercises are to inspire and keep you engaged on your feet doing things, not to read theory. So hop to it thespian! I had a lot of fun writing the Acting on Fire exercises. I hope you enjoy doing them.

# Exercise 1 "Levels of Intimacy" Enhances Your Focus & Camera Skills

I'm so excited you're here and have decided to keep your acting passion burning! To keep things varied you will find a variety of different exercises. Instead of doing three focus exercises in a row I'll mix it up a bit and sprinkle them throughout the 60 exercises.

That said, this book is yours! You can use it any way you want. For your convenience each chapter heading will include a title of the lesson plus the primary acting skill it covers. For the rest of you, there's nothing more to do. Just access each day from your phone, tablet or laptop and let's go!

**Step One:** Memorize the short monologue below:

Don't look back. You're not going that way. That's what she told me just before she walked out the door. Such simple advice. So simple. Why can't I follow it? I wanted to follow her. She's got her life all figured out.

**Step Two**: Find a place to sit next to a lamp. Turn out the lights and turn on the lamp as you sit beside it.

**Step Three:** Say the monologue as if you are speaking to yourself. There is no one outside the glow of the lamp. You have no one to communicate towards except yourself. Let the small area of light build a cocoon of intimacy around you.

**Step Four:** Repeat at least one more time.

**Step Five:** Do the entire lesson again only this time do it with the lights on. Resist the urge to do anything larger or look out across the distance.

**Step Six:** Repeat Step Five at least one more time.

**Step Seven:** Reflect on if anything felt different performing in the lamp light versus the fully lit room.

# Exercise 2 "Hitting Your Mark" Enhances Your Camera Technique Skills

Welcome back! Today we'll focus on the huge difference between hitting your mark on stage versus hitting your mark on camera.

First the similarity. One thing both stage and camera have in common is lighting for effect. If you walk too far downstage in a theatre you'll often be plunged into darkness as the lighting grid doesn't usually extend beyond the curtain line by much. While that may be great for a certain effect it's not so great if you're supposed to be clearly seen.

Likewise a camera shot is set up so the lighting will look a certain way when you hit your spot. Additionally when you're on set you also need to be in focus. Even a few inches can cause you to blur depending on the camera's depth of field.

While stage actors can approximate where they stand so they don't bump into other actors or moving sets, film actors have to land on their mark so they don't look fuzzy causing everyone to shoot the scene all over again. If there are dozens of extras and/or the camera is moving at the same time the actor is moving this is even more important.

No worries. Hitting your mark can be achieved simply. One way is to stand on your mark and then walk backwards while saying your line. If you walk the same speed backwards as you do forwards you should easily hit it every time.

But what if the director wants you to start farther back or closer forward? You can do the same trick but count your steps so you'll know how many to take. However, this option isn't ideal as it takes you out of character. Today's lesson offers a simpler way.

**Step One:** Place a piece of tape on the floor to be your mark.

**Step Two:** Stand on your mark. Look straight ahead and see if there's something you are aligned with.

**Step Three:** Turn your head and pick a piece of furniture or an item on the wall you can see that you are aligned with. You should be standing on your mark where the two imaginary lines intersect. If there's nothing directly aligned with you then you'll note if you're a couple of inches to the left or right of an item. (Note: Be sure to pick something on set that's not likely to get moved around. No lights, poles or director chairs!)

# Exercise 3 "A Day in Their Shoes" Enhances Your Character Development Skills

Today's exercise is short, simple and a lot of fun. Plus there are many variations you can try throughout the day wherever you are.

## Variation One

**Step One:** Choose a character. The character could be from a book, movie, current audition or someone completely made up.

**Step Two:** (Optional but highly recommended) Wear a pair of shoes this character might wear. Would it be comfy sneakers? Dress shoes? Workplace pumps?

**Step Three:** Practice sitting, standing and walking as this character.

## Variation Two

**Step One:** Same as step one above. Choose a character.

**Step Two:** Think about whether this is a more

intellectual character or a more animalistic, materialistic character.

**Step Three:** If the character is more intellectual practice walking around while leading with your head. If the character is more materialistic, practice walking around while leading with your hips and groin.

## Variation Three

**Step One:** Grab your iPod or cell phone with music on it and ear buds and head to your favorite walking spot.

**Step Two:** Take a walk. Each time the song changes make a small adjustment to how you walk. Maybe on some songs you bounce more. On others you glide. Explore different ways of moving as you walk. Let the music lead you.

# Exercise 4 "Listening with Both Ears" Enhances Listening and Focus Skills

Because "acting is reacting" it only makes sense to enhance your focus skills so you know when to react. Then your listening skills kick in so you know how to react.

Even though this exercise is done alone it does require a minimal amount of equipment that should be easy to find in most households. You'll need two objects that can play audio at the same sound level. Any of the following should work:

- Radio

- TV

- Cell Phone

- Tablet

- Computer

- MP3 Player with an external speaker

The two objects do not have to match. For instance you could use a cell phone with a TV. Or a radio with a computer etc.

Next you'll need to find something to listen to on

your devices that involves human speech. These could be a:

- Podcast

- Reality TV show

- News show

- Standup Comedy show

- The opening segment of a late night show

Choose anything you know that will include several minutes of just talking without being interrupted by musical scenes or long pauses of silence. (In this case TV shows and music would not work.)

You'll want something different on each device. For example you could use a podcast on MP3 player and a news show on your TV.

Last you'll need a timer. You could use your cell phone timer or if all else fails just keep a clock nearby to look at even though it may make the exercise a little harder.

Start by playing both devices and adjust the volumes until they match.

Set a timer for 5 minutes.

Begin listening to the device on your left for a little

while and try to pick out what's being said. Then switch to the device on your right and try to pick out what's being said. Keep going back and forth for a few minutes.

Now write down what you heard.

Were you able to pick out complete thoughts that made sense?

Try the exercise again and see if you can focus on even more complete thoughts.

# Exercise 5 "Memorize Using Your Ears" Enhances Your Memorization Skills

So why do I advocate memorizing with your ears? What does that mean anyway?

When I was working on my first big theatre role I had dialogue on about 40 pages of the script. And I did what a lot of actors do, I highlighted my lines in one color and underlined "trigger" words in the other person's lines right before it in another color.

(A trigger word is any word that would jog my memory about what my next line was. For example: Actor A says "I can't believe mom buried the cat under the dog house." And Actor B replies "I can't believe she buried it at all. She hated Whiskers with a passion!" The words "buried the cat" would trigger Actor B to remember that their next line would be about Whiskers' unfortunate fate.)

The trouble with doing this for a long passage of lines is that I would get used to how they looked on the page. The sight of the words would trigger my memory wonderfully. But take the script away and my memory was not as good. After all, it's the other actor's voice that you will respond to, not a written script.

Thus, I devised my own system that's helped a lot. You'll need your script and an audio device to record with. I use a highlighter just to help me not lose my place but it's totally optional.

I do one page at a time.

## RECORDING ONE:

First I record Actor A's lines in a voice that's clearly not mine. You can have fun with this. No one's going to be listening to this but you. You can do an impression of someone famous, speak in a foreign accent, or just make up a funny voice.

Second, I read my lines silently to myself and tack on a couple of extra seconds of silence.

Third, I read MY lines aloud in my normal voice.

I repeat steps 1-3 until I finish the page. Then stop the recording. If it's digital I might label the file "Page 1 with pauses and replies."

When I play it back I speak my lines during the silent pauses. What this does is allow me to be triggered by the other actor's lines, say my own lines out loud and then listen to my own lines right afterwards to see how close I was to getting the lines correct.

**Do this for all your pages before moving forward.**

**Keep practicing with these recordings, speaking aloud during the silent pauses until you get your lines right most of the time.**

## RECORDING TWO:

First I record the other actor's lines in a voice that clearly is not mine.

Second, I read my lines silently to myself and without the extra second or two of silence.

When I play it back I speak my lines aloud during the silent pauses.

**Do this for all your pages before moving forward.**

**Keep practicing with these recordings until the pauses seem a little too long.**

## RECORDING THREE:

First I record the other actor's lines in a voice that clearly is not mine and I record it while speaking the lines quickly.

Second, I read my lines silently to myself quickly.

When I play it back I speak my lines aloud quickly during the silent pauses.

Do this for all your scenes.

Keep practicing until you don't feel the need to practice them any more.

By going through this process, not only will I have memorized my lines, I will have memorized them the way they'll be triggered on set or on stage, by another actor's voice. Also, by the time I graduate through recording three I will have memorized them so thoroughly I can say them at any speed I need to fit the pace of the script!

# Exercise 6 "Remembering Sensations" Enhances Your Imagination Skills

If you've been studying acting for a while, one popular way to stir up emotions is to recall an emotional moment from your life that matches the emotion you need in a scene.

This exercise starts off similarly but then goes further so that you will not necessarily need to keep bringing up tragic moments in your past while doing a scene in the present.

First set a timer for five minutes.

During those five minutes remember an emotional memory from your life. It should be a strong emotion with high energy .

After the time is up, notice how you feel physically. If you were ecstatically happy did you feel lightheaded? If you were sad did you feel it more in your stomach or in your chest? Every person is different so there are no right or wrong answers.

If you don't feel anything, set the timer again and try again with the SAME emotion.

Today's exercise is really two exercises rolled into one.

First choose a piece of music that evokes a general mood.

While playing the music move your body to match the music. Close your eyes if you feel self conscious but open them if you start moving a lot and need to keep your balance!

When the music ends, take stock of how you feel. If you've stirred up a significant emotion, where is that emotion living inside your body?

Finally, once you've completed either of these two exercises keep the physical sensations in your memory. You can practice re-creating the emotions by re-creating the physical sensations from memory.

Now you can apply this to your scenes without having to re-live dramatic moments of your life again and again.

# Exercise 7 "Brrr.... The Cold Read" Enhances Your Audition Skills

The dreaded cold read. You've never seen the script but you're expected to sound natural and "gasp" somehow act out the scene with no prior homework on the script.

Relax. First of all, your fellow actors are all cold reading too so it's a level playing field.

Second of all, because you have so little time to prepare it wouldn't make much sense to give you a whole list of tips to try and remember in the precious few minutes you have before a cold read. In fact there are only two things I try to focus on in these situations.

**Prep Step:** Before you start your audition, Skim the page and pick out the "trigger words" spoken by another character that will cause a reaction in your character.

**Step One: Look up at the reader** and listen for those trigger words while they speak to you.

**Step Two:** Keep your finger roughly near your next line so you don't lose your place when you **react to the trigger word** and look down at the page to read your line.

So that's actually three steps but during the audition

you're only focused on two.

## Assignment to practice alone:

Read a news article online aloud reacting naturally to what you read.

Then read it again. Each time you read a new paragraph try to transition into the following emotions, one paragraph per emotion.

Happy
Deflated
Annoyed
Bored

Do the exercise again with a different article. This time choose four new emotions and do the same thing.

This exercise will prepare you for new directions that may be thrown at you during a cold read.

# Exercise 8 "Pressure to Relieve Pressure" Enhances Your "Relaxation Skills"

Imagine for a moment you have an audition today. You took deep breaths before you got into the car. And the traffic was busy enough you weren't really nervous while driving to the audition location.

You make it to the waiting room just fine, sign in with a nice production assistant and take a seat.

You look around the room and a small chill goes up your spine as you notice all these other people who look a lot like you. Maybe they're the same height and weight. Same age, eye and hair color. Your mind starts playing tricks on you and you're just sure they're all the next incarnation of Meryl Streep or Daniel Day-Lewis.

What happened to all those deep cleansing breaths you took before getting in the car an hour ago? Now every time you try to "deep cleanse" you feel like hyperventilating instead!

It's okay. There are other things you can do to center yourself.

One way is to use acu-pressure to center yourself. Set your phone timer for 1 minute and then press your middle finger between your eyes into the indentation where the bridge of the nose meets the forehead. Leave it there until the 1 minute is up.

Do you feel silly with your finger in the middle of your forehead?

Another good acupressure point is on your wrist. Find the point where your wrist becomes your hand. The point that creases when you bend your hand forward. Place the thumb of your other hand on that spot and press down firmly for 2 minutes. This one's especially good for releasing muscular tension in your body.

If you feel it mostly in your stomach when you get nervous then this third pressure point might be exactly what you need. Turn your wrist over and find the two tendons that run vertically down the middle. Now place three fingers of your opposite hand horizontally across your wrist. This is how far down you must go. You want to place pressure between the two tendons about three widths below your hand. Place pressure here for a minute or two to release stress in your chest and tummy.

Now you'll be able to face those audition nerves like a pro!

# Exercise 9 "Three Step Characters" Enhances Your Character Development Skills

I don't know about you but I love to watch an actor I love and completely forget the actor I'm watching. Being able to transform into another character is practically synonymous with good acting.

But on the other hand, we're also mesmerized by actors who are so completely in the present moment that they react in fractions of seconds and never perform anything the same way twice. (I'm referring to character here and not physical blocking. Always repeat the same physical actions if you're acting in front of a camera. Otherwise you will be a nightmare for the editor and may limit your chances of being hired again.)

So do we immerse ourselves into our characters with hours of analysis or do we just fly by the seat of our pants playing the scene instant by instant?

In the Three Step Character Exercise you focus on what's happening inside the scene, what it is your character wants, and how your character will go about getting it.

If that sounds too simple, keep this in mind. The persona you present on a first date is very different than the person you are when you're sick in bed with the flu. When you talk to your boss, you act differently than you do when someone cuts you off in traffic.

In other words, you're already focusing on what's happening in your life, what you want at any given moment and acting in certain ways to get it. You've been doing this "character" thing your whole life!

Today's exercise is to look at one of the monologue scenes you've been working on, close your eyes and imagine for a moment that it's happening right now where you are.

Feel it. See it. Smell it. Hear the sounds. Even taste it if there's something to taste.

Now imagine that it's happening to YOU. Now is it your first date you? Angry traffic you? Professional you? Relaxed on the couch you? Bring the appropriate version of you to the scene in your mind.

Open your eyes and act the scene as you.

# Exercise 10 "Climbing Intensity" Enhances Your Camera Technique Skills

I bet you can guess from the title alone what today's exercise might be. First I'll tell you what it's NOT.

Never try to do a scene with a particular ending in mind. Just because you get angry in the scene doesn't mean you're going to be yelling by the end of it. In the moment, you might feel icy cold and give them a deadly stare more powerful than any red faced yelling could ever be.

That's not what the climbing intensity exercise is about.

Instead it's about knowing how much is too much in front of a camera.

You'll need a camera and a monologue to do this exercise.

First, turn on the camera and make sure you're in frame and can be heard by the microphone.

Second, you'll do the scene at a very low intensity. Let's call this intensity one.

Next, you'll do the monologue again at a slightly higher intensity. This would be number two.

Keep doing the monologue again and again at a

higher intensity each time until you've done it about seven times.

Now watch the scenes and choose the ones that look the most genuine on camera.

Most of the time it will be one of the middle takes rather than the first or last take that looks the most authentic.

Keep in mind that different scenes require different energy. Sometimes the first or last take truly are the most realistic looking. The point of the exercise is not to think "bigger" or "smaller" for the camera, but to focus instead on your energy.

# Exercise 11 "Voice Yoga" Enhances Your Vocal Skills

Surprise! Today's exercise is not going to be a list of tongue twisters! Instead we're going to look at various ways to get your body ready to speak with resonance. It doesn't matter if you're a voice actor, theatre actor or TV and film actor you still want a responsive voice that does what you want it to do.

These exercises may help:

1. Start with a moist throat. Drink water throughout the day. If you must drink coffee in the morning follow it up with an equal amount of water. The same for alcohol. If you must imbibe then follow it up with water.

2. Neck rolls. Yes, being careful to go only as far back as it feel comfortable, do some very slow neck rolls. Do both clockwise and anti-clockwise.

3. Hum. Humming is so much better for your throat than clearing it. But you already knew that! Try humming while lying down to feel it fully through your body. Also try humming a scale up one note at a time and them back down the scale again.

4. While you're lying down take a moment to work on expanding your lung capacity. Take a

deep breath in and then hiss for as long as you can before running out of air. Take another deep breath and say the alphabet loudly and see how many letters you can say before running out of air.

5. A common exercise for singers is great for actors too! It's called a PTKT and it gets your tongue in on the act and ready to articulate. Just say "puhh tuhh kuhh tuhh" over and over again. Try alternating between fast and slow. Also try saying at higher and lower pitches.

6. Alright, alright, if you insist here's a tongue twister for you die hard twister lovers! "She stood on the balcony, inexplicably mimicking him hiccupping, and amicably welcoming him home."

7. If you really want to give your mouth a workout after all these warm ups read classic literature aloud. If you can read Shakespeare, Edgar Allen Poe or J.R.R. Tolkien aloud without stumbling, cold reading a modern script will be a breeze!

# Exercise 12 "Scene Synonyms" Enhances your Scene Work Skills

When you first read a scene it's usually pretty clear what a character wants. But if you go into an audition with only your character's want in mind you could be missing out on being memorable.

That's where actions come in. Sure you want a hot date, but how do you go about getting it? Do you flirt? Do you play hard to get? Do you pretend to be shy, always glancing up but never holding long eye contact?

All of the above are examples of using "actions" to get your wants. So let's take action!

Pick a scene or monologue you're working on.

Grab a pen or pencil and write in different actions you can try. You may not get your want at the end of the scene. Do you switch actions halfway through the scene? Do you try desperately to get what you want using the same action again and again only more intensely each time? That's your choice!

Sometimes a small change in how you word your action can create a slightly different performance from take to take. I've listed synonyms for the same action below.

Practice your scene five times. Each time choose one of these actions to do your scene. Then notice how your performance changed.

Proud and sure

Never wrong

Relaxed and charming

Slick confidence

Generous and Kind

# Exercise 13 "Moving Meditation" Enhances your Relaxation Skills

Most relaxation exercises tend to focus on your breath. If you've ever sat in an audition room and noticed folks breathing deeply with their eyes closed then you know what I mean. But sometimes I need to get all that excess energy "out" of my system.

In this exercise you can do almost anything physical as long as it involves some sort of steady rhythm. Take walking for instance. Stand up and walk around the building a few times. (You did get to your audition early didn't you? Make sure you set a timer on your phone so you'll be back in plenty of time.)

Now as you walk pick a steady rhythm. Notice how your feet feel as you put them down on the ground one after another. You're getting the energy out of your nervous stomach and into the ground. Add your arms. Let them swing in a steady rhythm. Lastly, if your breath isn't already steady, add it in a steady rhythm.

You don't have to reserve this for auditions only. Any time you get tense just about any rhythmic physical activity will do. This can help before auditions, before class, before a performance, before memorizing lines if you're not feeling focused, after your day job and before your practice time, and any time not related to acting when you might need to relieve a little stress.

# Exercise 14 "Memorize Backwards" Enhances your Memory Skills

If you've ever looked up tips and tricks to enhance your memory very often they work for memorizing a list or numbers but not so well with memorizing lines. I remember once memorizing a long list of items using quite an amazing story complete with elephants and unicorns and superheroes in it! While it was great for memorizing that list, I don't want to be thinking about unicorns when I'm doing a dramatic movie scene.

One technique I discovered that works especially well when you have a large block of dialogue or even a monologue to remember is to memorize backwards.

If you remember our previous memorization lesson I mentioned "trigger words" coming from the other actor's lines. But what if you're the only one speaking for a long paragraph?

Have you ever been on stage or on camera and everything starts off fine but halfway through you keep thinking what's next? OMG I hope I remember what's next!

When you memorize backwards you will have gone over the last line of that text a lot more often than the first line. This virtually eliminates the fear or forgetting what's next because the ending of the piece will be so thoroughly memorized.

Another plus side to memorizing backwards is that it helps keep you from getting locked into a line reading because the novelty of memorizing backwards keeps the lines fresh during the process.

Here's how you do it. Say you have to memorize the following lines:

Patricia said we have to get back before four. Personally, I think she's nuts because I wouldn't want to waste any precious daylight hours when we could be searching for Tom. He's so scared of the dark he'll probably go into hiding.

Here's how you might go about memorizing this backwards.

First you would memorize: "He's so scared of the dark he'll probably go into hiding."

Once you have that down you might break the next sentence into a shorter segment like this. "We could be searching for Tom. He's so scared of the dark he'll probably go into hiding."

Make sure you've got that part thoroughly memorized before going on.

Then keep going with: "I wouldn't want to waste any

precious daylight hours when we could be searching for Tom. He's so scared of the dark he'll probably go into hiding."

Got that in your head solidly?

Then: "Personally, I think she's nuts because I would want to waste any precious daylight hours when we could be searching for Tom. He's so scared of the dark he'll probably go into hiding."

Once that's all memorized well you're almost done!

Next: "Patricia said we have to get back before four. Personally, I think she's nuts because I wouldn't want to waste any precious daylight hours when we could be searching for Tom. He's so scared of the dark he'll probably go into hiding."

Voila! You're finished! Try memorizing backwards the next time you have a block of text to memorize and see if you find it easier that way.

# Exercise 15 "Walking A to Z" Enhances Your Focus Skills

Being present will help you focus on what your acting partner is actually doing and not on what you think they should be doing in the scene.

Today's exercise is an easy one and has the added bonus of being easy physical exercise as well. Simply go for a walk in an urban area and start looking for the letters of the alphabet in correct alphabet order...A...B...C... all the way to Z. This exercise helps you focus, keeps you in the present moment and coordinates this with physical movement. All of which will help you the next time you have to do a scene with another actor.

The bonus with this and all other focus exercises is you'll find your everyday life getting easier as well. When you're focused on the present you're not torturing yourself with past "shoulds" nor are you stressing yourself with future "what if's."

Happy walking A to Z!

# Exercise 16 "In the Woods" Enhances Your Character and Imagination Skills

If you're an onscreen actor you may find yourself acting to a post-it note on a green screen or to someone dressed in a motion capture suit that looks nothing like the alien creature you're interacting with in your script.

Today is sort of a secret challenge because you won't tell anyone what you're doing even though you'll be doing it while out and about in the regular world.

The challenge for you today is to either pretend you're an elf or a warrior, take your pick.

The first part of the exercise is to do everything like an elf or a warrior would. For example an elf would pad across a hallway stealthily and gracefully. Meanwhile a warrior would stride down a hallway with their head erect and tall.

The second part of the challenge is to imagine you're hunting in the woods. For example, if you're getting water out of a water cooler at work, you might imagine that it's a rock with a water spring rushing down the edge.

This can be a subtle exercise. No need to carry a bow and arrow or sword. The more believable your imagination can make it and the more believable you react to it the better.

Now the next time you face nothing but four walls painted green for CGI special effects you'll be prepared!

# Exercise 17 "Baby Toes" Enhances Your Focus Skills

This acting exercise is so freeing. I love doing this when I'm stressed out because it's also quite silly. If you live with significant others, roommates, family etc. you may want to close the door.

Okay, it's short, simple and sweet but very rewarding.

Young infants do not realize that when something moves past its line of sight that it still exists. This is why the game "Peek a Boo" is so popular for them. To them you exist and then you don't exist. This exercise forces you to look at the world with brand new eyes. And constantly "re-discover" things each time you look at them.

Step One: Set a timer for 5 minutes.

Step Two: Take off your shoes and lie down on the floor.

Step Three: Begin playing with your fingers and toes as if you've never seen them before.

Step Four: Look to your left and "discover" something for the first time. Examine it in every detail. Reach for it like a baby in a crib would.

Step Five: Look back up at your fingers and "discover" them all over again as if it's for the first time.

Step Six: Keep "discovering" things for the first time. You can re-discover your fingers and toes over and over again. Or look to your right and "discover" something new each time. Keep going until your timer goes off.

Now the next time you have to do 28 takes of a scene on set, or you get hired to do 28 shows a month in theatre, you'll be able to recall and focus on what it's like to "discover" the moments anew and put on a wonderful performance!

# Exercise 18 "Putting It Together 1" Memorization

Congratulations! You've made it through the first 17 exercises. My intention so far has been to offer you a variety of techniques to apply directly to work you're already doing.

But as acting work can be heavy one season and light the next, the next batch of exercises will focus on using some of these techniques together as a whole.

First here's a monologue to be memorized. I kept it short so that it could be memorized quickly and thoroughly so you can jump right into the follow up "Putting it Together" exercises right away.

Your exercise for today is to memorize the following monologue using either Exercise 5 and memorizing using a recording. Or exercise 14 and memorize backwards.

While saying the monologue you are opening a metal slab that's covering something underground inside a warehouse.

Get me a rope will you Sabine.

How do I even get into these situations?

I mean I seriously gotta get a day job where people aren't

so violent with their demands.

Like a nice cube farm job in customer service.

Someplace I can just answer the phone and help someone return a pair of sneakers they don't want.

Where my biggest decision of the day is what type of creamer to use in my coffee.

I like hazelnut by the way.

This whole shimmy down a dark hole into who knows what kinda slime ain't cutting it anymore.

Sabine, you got the rope yet?

Sabine?

# Exercise 19 "Putting it Together 2" Relationships

So now you should have memorized your monologue.

In today's exercise you'll want to ask yourself one main question. What is your relationship to things?

Normally you would have an entire script to come up with a few answers for this. But by not giving you a full storyline it allows you to practice your acting more by coming up with a few of your own to practice.

Try acting the monologue twice in each of the following scenarios:

Your relationship to the scene: You really don't want to dig into whatever's under that metal slab.

Your relationship to Sabine: She's your daughter.

Your relationship to the scene: What you're doing could save people's lives.

Your relationship to Sabine: She's your annoying co-worker.

Your relationship to the scene: You're determined to get to whatever's under there first!

Your relationship to Sabine: She's an intern learning from you.

# Exercise 20 "Putting it Together 3" Scene Work

Today you will make up obstacles for the character in your monologue scene.

Usually you would find them in the script but in this case we'll make up several for extra practice.

First do the scene as if bullets are flying past.

Second do the scene as if the metal slab is sinking away into a black hole.

Third, do the scene as if you barely have any strength left but you know it'll save the human race.

Now do the scene as if Sabine is your daughter and bullets are flying.

Next do the scene as if Sabine is your annoying co-worker and the metal slab is sinking into a black hole.

Next do the scene as if Sabine is your intern and you barely have strength to save the human race.

If you found the last three scenarios challenging, do them a couple of times until combining multiple things feels like second nature to you.

# Exercise 21 "Putting it Together 4" Music

This one's a little easier than exercise 20. Today we're going to apply elements from exercise 6 to your monologue.

Step one, pick out four pieces of music or songs with very different moods. It doesn't matter if they make sense for the monologue we're working on or not.

Step 1: Close your eyes, and listen to song number one.

Step 2: Act out the monologue without thinking about it.

Step 3: Listen to song number one again only this time think more about how the song could possibly relate to the scene.

Step 4: Act out the scene again.

Step 5: Finally, act out the scene one more time without thinking too much about it.

Repeat steps 1 through 5 with the remaining three songs.

# Exercise 22 "Putting it Together 5" Character

Today you'll be you as you do the monologue scene. By that I mean, you're not playing a different character in these scenarios, you're playing yourself as if you were in these scenarios.

Do the scene as if you just found out you got a raise.

Do the scene as if you just found out you got fired.

Do the scene as if you just found out you" have to share your house with a house guest for 6 months.

Do the scene as if you're dodging bullets but you just found out you got a raise. (I know this doesn't seem to make sense but it will help you be flexible.)

Do the scene as if Sabine was your intern and you just found out you have to share your house with a house guest. (Would it affect how you treat Sabine? It might not. You decide.)

Do the scene as if the slab were sinking and you just found out Sabine was pregnant.

# Exercise 23 "Putting it Together 6" Camera

This time you get to choose your scenario.

What's your relationship to what's under that slab?

What's your relationship to Sabine?

What's your obstacle to getting that slab open?

Do the scene once.

Now we'll pull from exercise 1. Turn off all the lights and turn on one lamp.

Go next to the lamp and do the scene as if you and Sabine were the only two people in the world. Same relationship to the slab, to Sabine and use the same obstacle.

Now turn on all the lights and do the scene again as if you were wide out in the open in the daylight. Same relationships, same obstacle.

Notice the difference in how each scene feels. The first was a camera closeup and the second was a camera wide shot.

# Exercise 24 "Putting it Together 7" Camera

Before you begin, set up a camera to record yourself. You might want to test it to be sure you're in frame and you can be heard well.

You are going to do the scene seven times. Each time you will ramp up the scene's intensity a tiny bit while recording video. Here is your scenario.

Do the monologue as if Sabine were your daughter, what's under the slab is radioactive and you're dodging bullets.

Once you've done it seven times, watch the video and choose your favorites.

# Exercise 25 "Putting it Together 8" Audition Skills

Go back through the past 6 exercises of Putting it Together Beginning level exercises. Choose one of the scenarios you liked doing the best and the one you liked doing the least.

Set up a camera at eye level when you are standing up straight. Make sure you can be seen and heard from the mid-chest up. Place a mark on the floor so you know where you were standing. Hit record.

Do the scene in the way you like doing it the best. But this time remain standing in one spot the whole time.

Do the scene in the way you like doing it the least. Remain standing in one spot the whole time.

Watch the video. This is how most audition tapes are made. Is there anything you could do differently in the scene to give it the same complexity as before when you could move around freely?

# Exercise 26 "Improv for All" Listening Skills

Have you ever watched an Improv show like "Whose Line is it Anyway?" and wondered how in the heck they can keep a sketch going for minutes on end? There's an Improv technique that's so famous even non-actors have heard of it. But what you may not realize is that we ALL use this technique in our everyday lives.

Even if you're not a great conversationalist in general there are usually a few close friends with whom we get along so well with that the chatter just flows anyway. It's likely because whether you know it or not you've been using the "Yes and..." technique.

This technique can not only improve your listening skills as an actor, it can improve your imagination skills, increase your conversational skills and boost your audition skills as more and more auditions require flexibility in the room once you get past the first video round.

So here's how it works.

Part one is the "Yes." It means much more than to agree superficially with whatever your scene partner says. No, you can't just agree and then turn around and contradict them. It means you agree with them and then act as if whatever they said was 100% true in ALL its implications.

For example in an Improv comedy sketch.

## DON'T DO THIS:

Actor A: I'm your mother but I'll never understand how you climbed out of your pod before you could walk.

Actor B: Mom, I climbed out of a crib, not a pod!

Actor B has said "yes" to being Actor A's child but not "yes" to whatever pod means to them. They've said "no" to the other part of the scene and the scene now has no place to grow.

## DO THIS INSTEAD:

Actor A: I'm your mother but I'll never understand how you climbed out of your pod before you could walk.

Actor B: Mom, you know I just love you so much I couldn't wait to get out of that pod. I didn't fit in with all the other peas. (This is an example of the "Yes" and the "And" because now the second actor has defined pod as "peas in a pod.") OR Actor B could have said, "Mom, you know I just love flying in the big boys and girls spaceship so much, I couldn't wait to get out of that silly ole baby pod."

Either way, NOW we've got funny material to play with. The "And" is to add to whatever the first persona has said.

To review... the Yes is to accept what someone says as truth and the "And" is to add to that truth by adding your own information. Your assignment: Step one: Listen closely to your conversations and other people's conversations and notice how often the ones that last follow the yes, and pattern. An argument can last too, but it's lacking in the "yes" department.

Step two: The next time you're feeling tongue tied (or even if you're not) try accepting what a conversation partner has said and then adding information based on what the other person has said.

# Exercise 27 "Singular Singing" Scene Study Skills

Today's exercise is all about meaning and objectives. Being able to focus, listen and react are all about appearing natural on camera or onstage. But an actor doesn't act in a vacuum, they act inside the confines of a story.

Today's exercise may sound simple on the surface but it requires a little bit of coordination and forethought.

First get a scene or a monologue you've been working on. If you're not currently working on something then you can use the monologue from the beginner "Putting it Together" exercises.

Next determine what your character wants in the scene. This is the objective.

Then keeping the objective in mind, focus on one word per sentence you would want to emphasize to communicate your objective.

Say the monologue out loud once while emphasizing those words.

Now choose a melody that you know well and sing the monologue while emphasizing those same words.

While singing it's often easier to emphasize certain

notes in the song, but if those notes do not fall on the important words inside your monologue you must resist the urge to emphasize them.

Now sing the monologue a second time only THIS time go ahead and emphasize the words that fall during the most dramatic notes.

Now without thinking about either song speak the monologue one more time.

Was there more variety in the monologue after singing it two different ways?

This exercise can also be done while cold reading a book of fiction.

# Exercise 28 "Interior Thoughts Part 1" Enhances Your Characterization Skills

Have you ever wondered how Oscar award winners manage to submerge themselves in their roles so deeply?

I believe it's because they go one step further than writing a character biography. It's one thing to write out all your character's hopes, dreams, likes and dislikes but it's another to apply them to your character's thoughts moment by moment.

This exercise will take some time, but once you're done it should help you experience what it's like to get submerged into a role.

For this lesson you'll need a movie script and a printer to print it out. There are many free screenplays available to download online. I'd advise you to pick any genre you want but preferably choose a movie you've never seen acted on screen. Also, pick a character that is a major role with plenty of scenes and lines. This exercise may take a couple of days to complete.

Step One: Download and print the script. There are many websites with scripts available. Or play a movie and write down the scene as you listen to it.

Step Two: Read the script with a highlighter and

highlight your character's dialogue, action descriptions and any time they're mentioned by any other character in the script.

Step Three: Write a character biography somewhere other than on the script. It could be in a notebook or on your computer etc. Include things like they're goals, hopes, dreams, weaknesses, obstacles, likes and dislikes.

Step Four: Go through every scene line by line. Between each line of dialogue write directly onto the script what your character is feeling and thinking from one moment to the next.

It will take some time to do this, but it's well worth it!

# Exercise 29 "Interior Thoughts" Part 2 Enhances Your Characterization Skills

Before moving on to this exercise you should have completed exercise 29 Interior Thoughts Part One. This means you should have a full character biography written including their hopes and dreams, fears, pet peeves, favorite and least favorite foods, anything and everything about them.

You should also have by now a screenplay printed out with the character scenes highlighted and notes between every line of dialogue (and action) about how the character feels about what they are saying and doing.

Normally this would take several hours to do. But by taking the time to go into so much detail you're now ready to bring them to life.

And by that I don't mean in the scene. I mean into real life!

I want you to go to a coffee shop, or go shopping, or a bar, or festival or any public place for at least an hour.

Let's say you go to a coffee shop. You should have a feel by now on what your character drinks. Would it be sweet? Would it be black? Would your character chat easily with the barista?

Would they avoid looking them in the eye? If so is it because they're shy? Or because they're afraid? Or because they don't want to get involved? (If it's the latter, would they wear sunglasses indoors?)

Would they be a generous tipper? Stingy? Cheap because they're poor or because they're condescending?

Don't just answer the questions. DO them. And the best part about this exercises, it's unscripted! You have no way of knowing if you'll bump into someone you know. (How would the character react if they bumped into someone in high school?)

You might encounter a rude person! Or an unusually nice one! You don't know. But by now you DO know your character. Your job today is to go out and BE them. For an hour. In a public place. Have fun!

# Exercise 30 "Vocal Yoga Pt. 2" Enhances Your Vocal Skills

We've touched briefly on vocal warm-ups before in an earlier exercise, but now I'd like to stress the issue of body alignment and how it affects your breath and therefore your voice.

Voice requires the entire body to get involved. You never know when you might be running uphill, fighting a criminal or climbing a fire escape all while saying your lines. And you have to be heard while doing so!

Tall and relaxed posture will correct all kinds of vocal issues. Think of it this way. Your head is one of the heaviest parts of your body resting on top of one of your body's thinner parts, your neck. Any time your head is pushed slightly forward all kinds of small muscles contract from head to toe to keep the rest of the body from falling forward with it. The same thing happens if your head is pushed too far backwards.

When your head sits in the middle of your neck, aligned with your center of gravity, aligned over your ribs, aligned over your hips with both feet planted directly under you, it should feel as if your skeleton is holding you up, not your muscles.

Try it now. Keep making subtle adjustments until your bones are keeping you in place and muscle tension is relaxed.

Most importantly this kind of alignment enables you to breathe (and vocalize) with maximum capacity.

If your neck feels tense, or you cannot tell if it's in alignment then move your head front and back and side to side OUT of alignment a tiny bit so you can feel when it's in the center.

Next, loosen your lips and make a "BRR" sound by vibrating them very fast.

Now warm up your throat by humming. It's much healthier for you hum rather than clear your throat. (Avoiding dairy on acting days also helps as dairy can form mucus in your body.)

Find something to recite. If it's a scene you're working on that's great but it doesn't have to be.

Put your voice through its paces.

1.) Read the piece and over articulate every word.
2.) Read it again very loudly.
3.) Read it again very softly.
4.) Read it again in a silly voice.
5.) Finally, read it normally and notice how your voice feels.

# Exercise 31 "Multiple Personalities" Enhances Your Character Skills

Have you ever thought about all of the personalities you have inside you?

And I'm not talking about the ones you pull out for acting class either.

I'm talking about who you are around your very best friend. Think about how easy it is to talk to them. How delighted you are to see them. How you feel around them. Your tone of voice you use with them. Repeat the following as if you were talking to your best friend. "Hey! It's so good to see you. I can't believe it's been this long!"

How did that feel?

Now pretend you're in the car driving along having a great time. Suddenly a car swerves into your lane nearly tapping the corner of your bumper and 2 seconds later they slam on the brakes forcing you to not only hit your brakes but swerve to make a split second lane change.

Repeat the following as if that just happened to you. "Hey! Did you just see that?! What the hell is that guy thinking! There were cars right behind me and we could've been killed!

How did that feel?

Now pretend you're at a party and you don't know anyone. You were in a hurry and had to go in your work clothes. Everyone around you is wearing high end gowns and suits. You wouldn't have come except your boss needs you to pick up something from the host. Two party guests come up to you and start speaking to you but you realize they think you're someone else.

Repeat the following as if you're at that party. "Hi. Thank you. I'm not sure you have the right person. I'm just here to pick something up from the host."

How did that feel?

Now, to apply this to a role. Reflect on how your voice, your body language and the emotions you felt all changed in each scenario.

You were YOU every time, but the way you held yourself with your best friend was different than with two strangers. The way you reacted to a bad driver was different than you reacted during an upscale party.

The point is, we all have different facets of ourselves that can be used to create an acting role.

The rest of today's exercise is to use a scene you're working on and read it and/or perform it as if you're talking to different people.

Perform it as if you're talking to your mother on a good day.

Perform it as if you're talking to your boss.

Perform it as if you're talking to a check out clerk at your local drug store.

Perform it as if you're talking to someone you have a massive crush on.

Perform it as if you're talking to your mother on a bad day.

# Exercise 32 "Your Life as a Scene" Enhances Scene Study Skills

What could be more "real" to you than your own life rather than a scene from a script? Today's exercise will focus on a scene from your own life. Part one is identifying your scene.

As you go about your regular day today, be aware of an activity you do for at least two minutes. It could be as simple as brushing your teeth. It doesn't have to be fancy.

Now once you have done that activity put it on your list for later when you've got time to do this acting exercise.

1. When you're ready to practice, start by remembering where you were. Try to imagine it in your mind. What was near you in your environment.

2. What time was it?

3. Where were you? Get specific. Country, city, home, room, corner of room

4. What had just happened before you started this activity?

5. What do you expect to happen after this activity?

6. What did you need at that moment?

7. What was in your way of getting (or doing) what you needed?

8. What did you do so you could get (or do) what you needed?

9. Now gather any props you need. This is NOT a mime exercise. If you need objects, gather them together now.

10.     Set a timer for 2 minutes.

11. Recreate the scene and if you make sounds, chuckle, whine, curse etc. it's perfectly okay and encouraged.

Practice this for at least 30 minutes!

# Exercise 33 "Your Former Life" Enhances Scene Skills

First choose a short piece of text to work with. It could be the very first lines of a scene, or a monologue or even a bit of dialogue from a novel.

If you don't have anything try memorizing this:

"I've got something to tell you but I'm not sure how to start. Wait, why are you looking at me that way?"

Once you've got it memorized move on to the next step.

Place a mark in the middle of the room you're working in. A post-it, a piece of tape, lined up between two paintings on a wall. You decide where you'll stand or sit.

Your character's life begins long before the camera starts rolling and unless it's a death scene, it will continue long after the camera stops. Or if you're a theatre actor, long before the curtain opens or closes. This exercise helps you enter a scene with more life before you even open your mouth.

Before doing the scene imagine you've just had a flat tire and had to get it fixed while standing outside in the blazing hot sun.

Now walk to your mark and deliver the line.

Did the scene you imagined happening before you delivered your line affect the way you walked to your mark or the way you said your line?

Try it again, only this time imagine you've just spent the last two hours being pampered by someone special.

Notice if anything changed.

Try it again and this time you just narrowly escaped being attacked by a stray dog.

Notice what changed.

Try it again and this time you've just come home from a boring lecture given by someone who really didn't care if anyone was listening or not.

Note your reactions.

Try it one more time only this time you've just made it through a grueling marathon. You feel exhausted but proud.

Notice any changes.

# Exercise 34 "Two Characters and Three Lines" Enhances Your Improv Skills

The more I study improv, the more I'm convinced its lessons can enhance any performance whether it's extensively scripted or not. Halle Berry who's known for scripted feature films and TV attributes improv as a key element of her acting training. Heck, that works for me!

So here's today's exercise:

First get in character and say one line of a situation.

Then immediately get into a totally contrasting character and deliver a second line.

Finally, go back to the first character and say the last line.

While doing all of this keep in mind the larger the contrast between the two characters the better. If one stands up straight as a superhero, try the second hunched in the gutter. If one speaks forcefully, have the second barely above a whisper.

And finally, see if you can do these scenes focusing on creating a who, what and where by the end of the three lines of dialogue.

It sounds simple but there's more to it than it might seem at first!

Once you get familiar with the exercise, go faster and switch faster until you're a master! Feeling like you got this? Now slow down a bit and try doing a three character scene.

# Exercise 35 "10 Minute Marathon" Enhances Your Improv Skills

So today's exercise will be a challenge but if you can make it all the way through without stopping the result will be worth it.

To do this exercise you'll need a timer of some sort and a monologue. First set your timer for 10 minutes.

Second, begin reciting a monologue you have memorized.

Then after about a minute morph the monologue into a two person scene and continue it until the timer dings. During this time you may revert back to the monologue as part of the conversation. You may leave the monologue alone and only use it as a starting point with who, what, and where. You can include flashbacks. You can jump to a related scene between these two characters. Just keep playing both characters until your 10 minutes is up.

The idea is to never stop for longer than a few seconds until something in your brain "clicks" and the scenes just flow continuously.

This isn't for the faint of heart, but helps teach both improv AND focus for when you're no longer acting alone and must stay with the dialogue of additional actors.

# Exercise 36 "Conjuring" Strengthens Your Focus Skills

This exercise has two parts and surprise.... you've already done one of them without knowing it!

First look around the room and find and notice an object with a decent amount of detail to it.

Next, set your phone timer for 5 minutes.

Immediately close your eyes and try to "conjure" the image of this object in every detail. Even hold your hand out and consider its size in relation to the palm of your hand. Is it heavy? Light? Bigger than your hand? Smaller than your hand. Keep going for the full 5 minutes with your eyes closed!

After the timer rings get the object (or if you chose a really large, heavy one, go over to the object and examine it for another 5 minutes (with your eyes open of course.)

Now set your timer one more time and try conjuring the item again in every detail.

When the time is up, how did you do?

The ability to recall and recreate things like this will come in handy on a film set when you're working against a green screen or have to re-shoot something weeks or months after the original scene was shot.

# Exercise 37 "Country Improv" Enhances Your Improv Skills

If you've ever done theatre you know when you're waiting in the wings and you hear your cue to go onstage. At that moment you don't have time to think "I'm not ready! Give me more time! I'm scared!" No, you hear your cue and you walk onstage and whatever happens. happens.

And if you've never been on stage then you could probably imagine it in your mind as you read the paragraph. Another example is dancing. You move when the musical beat tells you to move. You can't shy away from it or the dance falls apart.

All of this applies to film acting. If you spend too much time inside your head during a scene your performance will fall flat. Just because there's a camera there doesn't mean you can do a take 36 times. The director may want to do another angle and another. And maybe it WILL be 36 times when it's done, but only 7 of the takes looked good with the lighting and the camera moves. And your acting must look good during those 7 takes too! You don't want long pauses between conversational exchanges! You don't want to look like you're "deciding" how to react. You must think quickly on your feet.

And that's what this exercise is designed to do. It's so easy you can even do it in your car!

First you'll want to find a country music station on the radio. Country music is pretty famous for using predictable rhyme schemes in their songs and this is what you want.

Second, let the song play for a moment so you get the general melody of the song and rhythm down first. Then when a new verse begins, listen to the first line and sing out loud a totally made up one that rhymes!

Get as silly as you like with this! You can't shrink back. You've got to be on the ball and in the moment. Once you've got that down here's a second bonus exercise to try.

Tune your radio into an all talk station.

Listen to the DJ talk for about 30 seconds or so and switch the radio OFF while YOU finish their sentence out loud. Keep talking until you've finished a complete thought on the topic. Keep doing this and you'll find yourself debating the pros and cons of things, defending topics you know nothing about and having a blast the whole time.

The idea is to keep talking smoothly as if you ARE the DJ just finishing the radio DJ's sentences and paragraphs.

Bonus points if you can adjust your speech to sound a little bit like the same person!

# Exercise 38 "Observing Your Emotions" Enhances Your Observation Skills

A lot has been written about observing others around us. People watching comes naturally to most actors because you find gems to dissect, imitate or leave behind.

But not as much emphasis is given to observing our inner life as it is related to your physical life. And more specifically our emotions. While many scenes involve everyday conversations, at some point in your acting career you're going to have to get mad.

Or laugh on demand.

Or cry.

And while we can yell, or smile while moving our shoulders up and down, it's easy to see these things are insincere if they're not connected to genuine emotion.

So today's exercise is not about "thinking" about what we do when we feel something. And it's not about pretending to feel a certain way.

It's about staying alert over the next several days to what we feel. Your job in this exercise is to catch yourself in the middle of a strong emotion.

For example: The next time you get angry what do you notice about your body? Does your throat close up restrict the air through your throat? Do you move your arms sharply like knives slicing through the air? What does YOUR body do when you're so angry you could just explode?

As you can guess, this exercise could even take weeks before you cover every emotion. And it's likely you will experience strong emotions and forget to catch yourself in the middle of them.

Don't worry. The next exercise will still be sent tomorrow. Just keep trying to catch yourself and observe what you feel as each emotion comes up and do this as an ongoing exercise until you've observed a whole catalogue of emotions and your personal physicality that comes with them.

PART 2: Of this exercise is to practice recreating these physical sensations to trigger your emotions when you need them.

# Exercise 39 "Putting it Together Intermediate Level 1" Memorizing

Congratulations! You've made it through 38 days of exercises! You now have an arsenal of exercises you can pull out any time you're alone either without an acting study buddy or when you're on set and between classes.

The monologue you memorized for the beginner level was based on easy to understand, casual and current speech patterns popular in the United States. However, you won't always be playing characters from this century in North America. Even modern takes on old classics like "Pride and Prejudice and Zombies" had the actors speak the literary dialect and vocal patterns directly from the book!

The important thing to remember though, as odd as the following monologue might feel as you read it aloud for the first time, you still need to connect to the words just like they are modern, casual ones from your own hometown.

Today's exercise is to memorize the following monologue using either Exercise 5 and memorizing using a recording. Or Exercise 14 and memorizing backwards.

"It is impossible to pinpoint when first the idea entered my mind.

But once conceived there was no halting it.

I made up my mind to sneak forth into the garden, turned the latch at the iron gate and opened it, ever so stealthily.

I crept undetected under the trellis and hearkened for telling footsteps.

Once the silence comforted me, I pulled a small vial out of my coat pocket.

There at my feet slept Cecily.

My neighbor's cur, a vile wretched thing.

She was always barking and gnashing her teeth at me.

I cleverly dissolved the vial's contents into her watering bowl.

Cecily vexes me no more.

And to this day, no one suspects my secret deed.

Except you now will know it no more.

For you have eaten as Cecily drank and will soon suffer the same fate.

# Exercise 40 "Putting it Together Intermediate Level 2" Relationships

Hopefully you're well on your way to having yesterday's monologue memorized. It's okay if it's not quite there yet as the language is harder to get a handle on at the intermediate level.

Because relationships are integral to all human drama, the first thing we'll explore is your relationships in the monologue.

Try acting the monologue three times under each of the following situations:

Your relationship to the scene: You work for the ethical treatment of animals.

Your relationship to Cecily: You're so fed up with Cecily you can hardly see straight!

Your relationship to the scene: You adopt every stray dog you see.

Your relationship to the person you're telling the monologue to: You're talking to Cecily's owner.

Your relationship to the scene: You're a cat person.

Your relationship to the person you're telling the monologue to: You're talking to your neighbor's lawyer.

# Exercise 41 "Putting it Together Intermediate Level 3" Scene Work

A scene has no drama without obstacles! The obstacle of not getting caught poisoning Cecily in the middle of the night is the obvious obstacle for this scene. But let's play with more.

First focus on the scene as written. Focus on not getting caught by the neighbor.

Second, do the scene as if Cecily keeps snorting about to wake up.

Third, do the scene as if someone appears to be watching you from across the street.

Fourth, do the scene as if the person you are talking to was actually there with you. Adjust phrases to say "remember when" or "and then we" etc.

Fifth, do the scene as if you keep stepping on sticks, gravel, squeaky dog toys and other things that make noise.

Finally, do the scene as if you are in broad daylight.

# Exercise 42 "Putting it Together Intermediate Level 4" Interior Monologue

It may sound funny to create a monologue for a monologue but here's how it works. This exercise focuses on what you were thinking about during the events as they happened.

First take out a blank sheet of paper and write the monologue down leaving a nice space between every single line.

Then write down what you as the character is remembering while the events were happening.

Then read the first line of your "interior" monologue to yourself.

Then read the first line of the original monologue out loud.

Then read the second line of your "interior" monologue to yourself.

Then read the second line of the original monologue out loud. Keep repeating this until you've completed the entire monologue.

Finally, read everything to yourself as a whole.

Then say the entire monologue aloud from start to finish.

# Exercise 43 "Putting it Together Intermediate Level 5" Mood Music

First pick out four pieces of music or songs with very different moods. Try to choose one that fits the mood of the scene. Then it doesn't matter if the other three songs make sense for the monologue as written.

Step 1: Close your eyes, and listen to song number one.

Step 2: Act out the monologue without thinking about it.

Step 3: Listen to song number one again only this time think more about how the song could possibly relate to the scene.

Step 4: Act out the scene again.

Step 5: Finally, act out the scene one more time without thinking too much about it.

Step 6: How did that feel to you?

Step 7: Repeat steps 1 through 5 with the remaining three songs.

Step 8: Did your performance after one of the songs that didn't seem to "fit" work out better than your thought it would? (It's okay to say "no." The idea is to be flexible.)

Step 9: Listen to the song that "fits" one more time and then act out the monologue.

# Exercise 44 "Putting it Together Intermediate Level 6" Camera Skills

Today you will need to set up a camera to record yourself. Before you go further, be sure you're in frame and you can be heard well.

Today you will be performing the scene seven times. During each performance you will ramp up the scene's intensity a tiny bit while recording it on video.

Here is your scenario.

Do the monologue as if you adore most dogs, Cecily keeps twitching like she's about to wake up and you keep stepping on things that crunch or make noise under your feet.

Once you've done it seven times making the scene a little more intense each time, choose which one felt the best to you.

Then watch the video and choose which one looks the most realistic to you.

Then note if it's not the same answer both times, how far "up or down" the intensity scale produced the most realistic result.

# Exercise 45 "Putting it Together Intermediate Level 7" Camera Skills

Go back over the intermediate level exercises and choose which relationships and obstacles you enjoyed performing the best and use them to answer the questions below.

What's your relationship to Cecily?

What's your relationship to your neighbor?

What's your obstacle to getting the contents of your vial into Cecily's drinking dish?

Do the scene once using the answers to all three of those questions.

Now turn off all the lights in the room you're in and turn on one lamp.

Go sit or stand next to the lamp and do the scene as if you and the person you're telling your story to were the only two people in the world. Same relationship to Cecily, your neighbor and use the same drinking dish as an obstacle.

Now turn on all the lights and perform the same scene with the same relationships and obstacles. Only this time do it as if you were in a wide open space.

Notice the difference in how each scene feels. The first was a camera closeup and the second was a camera wide shot.

# Exercise 46 "American Accents" Enhances Your Dialect Skills

So what is the Standard American Accent? Some might say it's the accent newscasters use.

A better question would be, IS there a standard American accent?

And the true answer is "no." British actors learn a "standard" American accent, but if we're being honest no one could point to a single state in the United States and say "There! That's the state! That's where proper American speech is used."

Years ago, I got on a John Cusack kick and watched a bunch of his films in a week. When I got to the film "City Hall" I knew something was up. After watching a week of his movies, I was so used to hearing him speak in his natural speech I was tipped off immediately when he wasn't. But here's the weird part, I couldn't quite put my finger on it. Everyone else in the movie was from New York, but it was obvious he wasn't talking like the rest of them.

It turns out his character was from Louisiana. Now, folks, I'm from Louisiana. Deep, south Louisiana. And I've heard actor after actor slaughter the Louisiana dialect and make us sound like we're from Texas or Tennessee or most often... Georgia. For better or worse, when an actor is told their character is southern, a good many of them learn the Georgian accent.

But my point is NOT that he learned to speak in a thick, Cajun accent. Quite the opposite. See I lived in a medium sized city at the time. I had an accent but it's not the accent from deep within the swamps, spoken hundreds of years ago.

And that's where Mr. Cusack is a good example for all of us to emulate. He spoke with a "hint" of a Louisiana accent. So subtle that I knew he wasn't talking like he did in his previous movies, and also, so subtle it sounded perfectly natural to a native speaker of the area. He spoke with the "flavor" of the accent. He didn't drown his entire performance in Cajun hot sauce!

So today, I'd like to focus on the differences between the various regions of the U.S. and how you can add a bit of "flavor" to them in a role.

First, unless you're doing a broad comedy, you'll mostly want to go for the flavor of the region's accent.

Second, you'll want to learn the signature sounds of an accent. These are what make an accent distinct.

Third, to listen to the most authentic speech patterns of a region, rent an independent movie made in that region. Hollywood may or may not over exaggerate an accent for one reason or another.

(Especially in a comedy.) If you want to be praised for your authenticity, listen to the actors who live in the region.

You could go down the internet rabbit hole for hours looking up signature sounds of various U.S. dialects, so I've included a few here. Your task for today is to read a couple of pages aloud while speaking with these signature sounds.

Boston: The long "a." Park the car and take out the garbage." Sounds like "Pahk the cah. And take out the Gahbahge."

Connecticut: Drop the letter "d" when it comes in the middle of a word. A tandom bicycle becomes tanom bicycle.

Pennsylvania: The plural you is "yinz."

South: The plural you is "y'all'." The contraction of the words "You" and "All" becomes "Y'all." Pronounced Y-AW-L.

Wisconsin: Add a "t" to the ends of words that end in double "s." Lacross becomes Lacrosst.

Read two pages using the Bosotn long "a."

Then rent an independent movie from a region you're interested in and stop it from time to time to repeat some of the dialogue.

# Exercise 47 "Playing Drunk" Enhances Your Layering Skills

I wasn't quite sure what to call this lesson as "acting drunk" seemed like a one of a kind issue in a production, but the main lesson to learn is that being "drunk" doesn't negate all the character work you do.

All drunk people are not the same.

And "acting drunk" means you layer "being drunk" on top of all the other scene work you do.

Because there are a variety of ways to "act drunk" I'd like you to pick a scene to practice with. It can be the first or second monologue of this course, if you do not have a script you're reading currently.

Do the entire scene or entire monologue all the way through trying out each of these techniques.

One thing to keep in mind at all times is that drunks try to cover up their drunkenness. They want you to think they're sober. So unless you're going for broad comedy, always keep these sober attempts in mind.

1. Allow yourself to mentally process things more slowly and let your motor skills be half as tense as they normally would be.

2. Do the scene while walking slowly, but allow your knees to feel rubbery as you try very hard to keep

87

yourself moving in a straight line.

3. Let your speech rhythms be erratic. Short bursts and languid vowels in the same sentence.

4. Attempt to keep your focus on a single spot on the wall as if you were having trouble seeing the wall.

5. Ask yourself what kind of drunk (angry, happy, sad) your character would be and exaggerate those emotions.

6. Play the opposite emotion of the one you just played.

7. Set up a camera and do all of the above again.

8. Which of these techniques worked for you the best?

# Exercise 48 "Being in Love" Enhances Your Layering Skills

At first glance playing a love story or a romantic comedy might seem less intimidating than a huge action film or horror film.

But then you realize, you're not in love with the actor who is playing opposite you. In fact, you're anything but and the camera will pick up every little nuance to give you away.

And what about the big kiss of true devotion and passion at the end? Or lots of getting to know you kisses in the middle?

Here are a few things you can prepare in advance alone. Along with some tips to keep in mind when you see your scene partner.

Kissing:

1.) Discuss any areas you feel uncomfortable with ahead of time. If they kiss your neck and you flinch the scene is ruined.

2.) This is one of those rare times when acting impulses have to be curbed. Once some physical boundaries are set don't deviate from them during a scene "on impulse." If the butt is off limits don't suddenly grab it because you were "in the moment."

3.) Unless it's very typical of the character, no closed

mouth kissing. Closed mouth kissing almost never looks real. Open mouth, no tongues will look much more authentic. (Always discuss this before hand!)

4.) Keep vitamin C handy throughout the rehearsal period when you are kissing. Do not practice a kiss while you are sick. Let everyone know in advance if you will not be able to rehearse a kiss that day.

Alone Preps for Falling in Love:

1.) Think about someone you're in love with. And then practice the scene.

2.) Find a photo of someone you have or had a crush on. Tape it on the wall at eye level. Then do the scene.

3.) Look at a photo of your co-star and no matter how much or how little you get along, choose one physical aspect you like about them. Close your eyes and really focus on it for 2 minutes. Open your eyes and do the scene. (You can also tape a photo of them at eye level on the wall.)

4.) Find out if the two of you have something in common you both enjoy. The next time you do that thing, imagine them with you enjoying it too.

On set:

Remember numbers 3 and 4 of your falling in love preps and then enjoy the scene!

# Exercise 49 "Parenthood" Enhances Your Layering Skills

Like the previous lessons whenever you're asked to play a parent you're more than just a parent. You still have to look at the character's needs, wants and objectives outside of being a mother or father. Then you layer parenthood on top of that in scenes involving your kids even if it's only talking about them when they are off screen or off stage.

The way to create a connection with the actor playing your child is to actually think back to when you were a child and think about yourself.

Think about all the hurts and joys of your own childhood days for a minute.

Then hone in on the hurts, disappointments, frustrations for a few minutes until you can pull those memories and emotions up with ease.

The next time you're on set or on stage, pull up these memories while looking the actor who is to play your child directly in the eyes. You want to feel like they are an extension of yourself. They are the younger version of you.

Only this time you get to protect them and guide them away from harm. They may not follow your lead, but this instinct to protect our younger, innocent selves not only mimics the way parents feel towards their kids, it will also help you bond with the younger actor during scenes.

Remember to look them in the eyes while doing this. Even though this might seem like a two person exercise, you really do all this prep work beforehand on your own, and then look at a kid in line at the grocery store. Or at a coffee shop etc.

Often they can feel this warmth and protectiveness that comes up from you and you may just make a new little friend for a few moments.

# Exercise 50 "Vocal Gymnastics" Enhances Your Vocal Skills

You don't have to be a voice actor to benefit from voice over and voice acting exercises. The more flexible you can be with your voice the more prepared you will be when faced with characters written in the script with specific vocal traits.

Today's exercise is actually two exercises.

1.) This first one can be kind of strenuous on the voice. Watch something animated for about 5 minutes. Then mimic one of the character's voices for about 5 minutes. Drink some water and do something nonverbal to rest your voice for a bit.

Then do it again and mimic one of the other character's voices for 5 minutes. Then drink water and rest your voice.

Once you're comfortable doing both voices, read a scene between two people and assign each character a voice.

Read the script switching back and forth between the two voices. Keep drinking plenty of water.

Bonus Exercise:

1.) Write down the names of your immediate family and on through your aunts, uncles and grandparents.

2.) Pick one family member and meditate on how they sound for a minute.

3.) Read a scene or monologue imitating their voice.

4.) Take a drink of water and do it again with another family member.

# Exercise 51 "Emotions in the Air" Enhances Your Emotional Skills

While emotions are an important part of an actor's trade, they cannot be forced or it will look false.

And while you could dig deep for some psychological triggers during an intense scene sometimes you can find emotions from the outside in.

What if the air around you were filled with an emotion? For example, what if you walked into an enormous mall in a large city with hundreds of people bustling by you with shopping bags and young kids scattering around them darting in and out of all the shoppers?

What was your emotional reaction to that scene?

No imagine you are out in the country on a moonless night. All you can see around you is flat land with a line of trees far off into the distance. The steady drone of crickets drown out any other noises other than the crunching of grass beneath your feet. Overhead you see too many stars to count in the black sky.

What was your emotional reaction to that scene?

Was it different?

Now choose your own environment and imagine the

air filled with it just like the air was filled with mist. Except in the examples above it might be filled with chaos (the mall) or peace (the country.)

Do not imagine moments before or objectives or any other acting technique. Just focus on the environment around you.

THEN notice the reaction inside you to the imaginary environment outside of you.

Once you get good at that, speak a monologue or simply make up words and movements it's up to you. The most important part though, is to stay in harmony with the environment around you as you talk and move.

Now try filling the "air" with love.

Once you feel it and have a reaction to it, move and speak in harmony with it.

Now try filling the "air" with mystery.

Once you feel it and have a reaction to it, move and speak in harmony with it.

Now try filling the "air" with decrepit, rickety old things.

Move and speak in harmony with it.

Come up with two more on your own and continue the exercise.

This is a subtle way to enhance the emotions of your character.

# Exercise 52 "Let's Get Active!" Enhances Your Scene Work Skills

Let's say you're working on a scene and in it, your character wants the other character to give you their coffee.

How you go about doing that without changing the dialogue is called an "action."

So today, grab your favorite two person scene!

Record the scene on your phone reading the other character's lines aloud while leaving blank spaces between for your own dialogue. (HINT: If you mouth your dialogue silently, you should allow the right amount of time since we usually read much faster when our mouths are closed.)

Then determine what your character wants in the scene.

Now go through the list below and do the scene once each time while using the "action" to get what you want. Some of these may seem subtle but even tiny changes in delivery can make a difference, especially on camera! And don't worry of the action does not seem to fit the scene. The idea is to explore possibilities.

You do not have to do all of these in one sitting. Start with 5 to begin and if you want to do more you can.


This exercise can be done again and again.

1.) I cajole you.

2.) I admonish you.

3.) I incite you

4.) I beg you

5.) I seduce you

6.) I bully you

7.) I lecture you

8.) I accuse you

9.) I apologize to you

10.) I soothe you

11.) I examine you

12.) I intimidate you

13.) I protect you

14.) I impress you

15.) I flatter you

16.) I mock you

17.) I tempt you

18.) I make you laugh

19.) I surrender to you

20.) I hurt you

# Exercise 53 "Fairy Tale Story" Enhances Your Imagination Skills

Keeping in mind the famous adage that acting is being truthful under imaginary circumstances we will do one more exercise to sharpen your imagination.

First choose a character from a fairy tale you know very well.

Now close your eyes and imagine the entire story from beginning to end.

Next imagine the entire story while adding more details of your own desire. Make the story more complete than the original story. Make if it's a little odd, make it even odder. If it's very dark, make it sweeter or make it darker, your choice.

Keep playing with this fairy tale coming up with new, detailed takes on it for several days.

Once you're really good at this, try to create your own fairy tale from scratch.

Repeat all the steps above adding more and new details from beginning to end over a series of days.

# Exercise 54 "Putting it Together Advanced Level 1" Memorizing

When I was very young I took ballet classes quite seriously. By the time I was a teenager I was on the path to becoming a professional ballerina. And as a teenager I was also given the opportunity to try out for our high school dance line.

While some dancers struggled to do high kicks without putting all their weight on the arms of other dancers I did it with ease. Ballet dancers do them all the time using their own balance without another dancer anywhere near them.

Spins? Got it!

Keeping your toes pointed? Second nature.

In the dance world, ballet is like Olympic training. If you're good at ballet, most other forms of dance become child's play.

I used to think Shakespeare was for theatre actors only. Until I became an actor.

That's when I realized, Shakespeare is like ballet. It's the Olympics for actors.

If you can maintain a character, speak with meaning and react truthfully in the moment with another actor while reciting Shakespeare, then doing modern auditions will be a cinch by comparison!

So your advanced monologue will be Viola from Twelfth Night. Even if you're a man! And here's why...

In the play the character Viola is dressed as a man named "Cesario" to serve in "Orsino's" court. Orsino loves Olivia, but Olivia loves Viola because she thinks she's the man Cesario.

Back in Shakespeare's day women were not allowed to perform onstage. So men played the female roles as well.

Whether you choose to play the monologue as a woman or whether you play the monologue as a man does not matter. What matters is the monologue is about unwanted attention from Olivia.

Use your favorite memorization technique to learn the monologue.

VIOLA: I left no ring with her. What means this lady?

Fortune forbid my outside have not charmed her.

She made good view of me; indeed, so much

That, as me thought, her eyes had lost her tongue,

For she did speak in starts distractedly. She loves me sure; the cunning of her passion

Invites me in this churlish messenger.

None of my lord's ring? Why, he sent her none.

I am the man. If it be so, as 'tis,

Poor lady, she were better love a dream.

Disguise, I see thou art a wickedness

Wherein the pregnant enemy does much.

How easy is it for the proper false

In women's waxen hearts to set their forms!

Alas, our frailty is the cause, not we,

For such as we are made of, such we be.

How will this fadge? My master loves her dearly;

And I (poor monster) fond as much on him;

And she (mistaken) seems to dote on me.

What will become of this? As I am man,

My state is desperate for my master's love.

As I am woman (now alas the day!),

What thriftless sighs shall poor Olivia breathe?

O Time, thou must untangle this, not I;

It is too hard a knot for me t' untie.

# Exercise 55 "Putting it Together Advanced Level 2" Trigger Words

If you've ever been to a bad Shakespeare play you've likely heard people speaking their lines in a continuous rhythm almost as if they were rapping instead of speaking. No amount of "speaking dramatically" will compensate for not understanding what you're saying.

Shakespeare's words are poetic and they all mean something.

Today's exercise is to focus on trigger words. You will want to print out the monologue and either underline or highlight the words in a sentence that trigger the idea or ideas in the next group of sentences.

Next go through the monologue until each line has meaning for you.

# Exercise 56 "Putting it Together Advanced Level 3" Emotional Wheel

Now that you've memorized the monologue and given each line meaning, it's time to layer on emotions.

First to make things easy, read the full dialogue as if you were bored with the whole situation.

Then recite the full monologue as if you were happy! You must provide your own reasons to justify this happiness.

Next recite the monologue as if you were deflated.

And finally, recite the monologue as if you were annoyed.

Now, do the first half of the monologue as if you were happy and the second half as if you were deflated.

And finally do the first half of the monologue as if you were bored and the second half as if you were annoyed.

Now do the monologue without attempting any particular emotion. Let the meaning of the words lead you to feel or not feel whatever you do. THIS IS WHAT YOU WOULD DO IN A PERFORMANCE.

As always, these exercises are to loosen you up and gain access to your emotions. Once you can access them easily the final performance should always be in the present moment letting emotions flow as they will.

# Exercise 57 "Putting it Together Advanced Level 4" Characterization Scene Work

Remember that long list of actions you worked through about a week ago? Now is your chance to put them into action again.

The next time you perform your monologue try doing it as if you were quite charming and you know you're charming. Write down any actions you could do to convey this and perform the monologue.

Then go again and write down any actions you could do if you were convinced you were never wrong. Then perform the monologue.

Try actions for meek and unsure.

Then do actions for proud and sure.

Finally, choose actions you think fit the monologue line by line or every couple of lines. Write them down next to the lines. And perform the monologue with those actions.

# Exercise 58 "Putting it Together Advanced Level 5" Scene Work

Remember when we talked about how your character's life begins long before the camera starts rolling and unless it's a death scene, it will continue long after the camera stops.

This exercise will help you kick off your scene with more life.

Start by putting a mark on the floor of the room you're practicing in. A piece of tape works well, or even a post-it note. (HINT: Remember when we talked about standing on your mark and looking around the room at eye-level so you can figure out where to stand without looking down. Figure this out first before continuing.)

Before doing the scene imagine you've just run into Olivia a few moments ago. Remember it's Olivia's lovelorn attention you do not want.

Now walk to your mark and deliver the monologue. You can continue walking around the room if you like. Pretend you're doing a scene not an audition.

Did thinking about the character Olivia before you delivered your line affect the way you walked to your mark or the way you said your line?

Try it again, only this time imagine you've just

bumped into Orsinio the man who loved Olivia.

Notice what changed.

Try it again and this time you were running down the hallway with intense excitement!

Notice what changed.

Try it again and this time you feel you were just rejected by your would be love.

Note your reactions.

Try it one last time, only this time you create your own imaginary moment before based on what you know about the monologue.

# Exercise 59 "Putting it Together Advanced Level 6" Multiple Approaches

Our time together is almost done and if you've been doing the advanced level putting it together exercises you're ready for some Olympic style acting workouts.

Today we'll compare multiple approaches so you can whittle down which techniques work for you the best.

First, print out Viola's monologue on a sheet of paper. Between each line write down her interior thoughts and/or emotions about each line.

Put the paper aside for now.

Next, go into your closet and find a pair of shoes Viola might wear. No need to go shopping, just find something to approximate the feeling of being Viola.

Put the shoes aside for now.

Now choose a piece of music Viola may have listened to in her day. Play the music and let your body, sway, move or even dance until the music's over.

Now perform the monologue.

Then put on the shoes you selected and do the

monologue again.

Finally, pull out your sheet with Viola's thoughts on it. Read over the thoughts quickly. Put the sheet away and do the monologue again.

Did any of the monologues feel better than the others?

BONUS: Go through all of these again while recording yourself in front of a camera.

# Exercise 60 "Putting it Together Advanced Level 7" Multiple Approaches Part 2

Wow! Can you believe it? You've made it through 60 exercises! You're an acting rock star and should be very proud. It's quite an accomplishment!

If you haven't taken action on all 60 yet, it's okay. Life happens. Things get in the way. But now you have a whole arsenal of techniques you can pick and choose from whenever you're alone, your scene partner's away or you simply aren't able to get to a group acting class.

Without further ado, here's your final advanced level acting exercise.

First we're going to combine three acting techniques all at the same time. I want you to perform Viola's monologue as if you're excited, using the actions proud and sure as if you just bumped into Olivia a moment ago.

Got all that? Good! Time to perform your monologue!

Done? Now erase all of that and start again. Before you start, I'd like you to look over the sheet of Viola's thoughts. Just read it through and put it aside. Now perform it as if there is the feeling of "mystery" in the air.

Done? Good. Let's go again.

Erase all of the above. This time let everything go and perform the scene letting it flow from moment to moment.

If you'd like to go again, pick an emotion, an action and a moment before. Then perform the monologue using all three at once.

Then, do it again by choosing a new environment around you.

Then, let everything go and do it one more time focusing purely on the present moment.

You are amazing! It takes a lot of grit to make it in the acting profession but by doing all 60 lessons consistently you've been building up your grit muscle day by day.

I hope all your acting dreams come true.

Much Love ~ Julie

# BONUS TECHNIQUES TO CRY ON DEMAND

I know crying on cue can be daunting. The first indie film I did where I had to cry on cue I thought I pretty much had it figured out. But then the day came... I tried three of the tips below before I found the one that worked for me personally.

Then I discovered at a later date the tip I used on that particular day wasn't fool proof. So I tried one of the other tips. And it works for me almost 100% of the time.

So enough about me, this is about YOU. I strongly urge you to try out as many of these tips as you need until you find the perfect fit for you. Just as not everyone cries at the same things in life that are legitimately sad, getting yourself to cry during a scene when honestly you woke up in a pretty great mood that morning can be a challenge.

Go forth and experiment! And when you find your secret to crying on cue, remember where you found it and send me a silent smile. I promise I'll feel the good vibes and be proud of your success.

Here are your tips!

**PRE-TIP:** On a day you have to cry a lot make sure you drink a lot of water and keep hydrated! This helps all the tips work better. (And contact lens wearers be sure your lenses are naturally moist especially if there are fans blowing air around. There's nothing worse than working up tears only to have your dried out lenses soak them all up before they fall.)

**TIP 1:** Working from the inside out. This one is the most intuitive one that many actors automatically go for first. Recreate a sad memory from your life in your mind. Run through every detail including what you see, hear, feel and even taste and smell if they apply. If nothing comes then tweak the memory a bit in your mind altering any of the 5 senses until the tears come.

**TIP 2:** Working from the outside in. Similar to the one above except instead of focusing so much on the memory, focus on your posture. The way your body felt. Recreate any physical sensations you remember. Hot eyes, tight muscles across the forehead, lead in your tummy, whatever the physical sensations are for you when you cry. Focus on those until the tears come. One thing to remember about this tip. It may feel artificial the first time you try this one. It's a tip to practice day after day until the tears come naturally. So don't wait until the day of shooting or performing to try this one out.

**TIP 3:** Vocal tics. This one's close to tip 2 except it focuses more on your throat. When you cry your throat constricts. Try to recreate that tight throat feeling. Then breathe deeply in as you get bits of words out. Try speaking in fits and starts. Stutter a bit. This can start a cascade of physical sensations causing you to cry real tears.

**TIP 4:** A physical momento. When my father passed away someone gave me a little metal rose. It's a physical representation of that era of grief. If you have a personal object that you associate with sadness you can bring with you then do so. If you can put it in your character's pocket and touch it between takes even better. If the object is too large, try taking a photo of it and looking at it between takes.

**TIP 5:** Losing the opposite. Maybe you're too young to have suffered a great loss in your life yet. In this tip you think of memories with someone you care about a lot. Then think about what it would be if they were suddenly gone from your life. Really let that sink in. Then let the tears come.

**TIP 6:** A little dab of irritation. If the scene calls for tears at the very start of a scene you may not have to go through all this emotional turmoil before stepping on set. Hollywood makeup departments have menthol lipsticks as well as eucalyptus blowers etc. to either waft in the air near your eyes, or dab on the skin under your eyes. If you're working on a theatre production or on a small budget indie film you can approximate this with a tiny dab of hand sanitizer on your fingers and wave them UNDER your eyes. NEVER IN your eyes! And never on the skin. Just in the air around your eyes.

**TIP 7:** Kindness to others. Sometimes we care more about what happens to someone else than we do about ourselves. If you've tried some of the other interior approaches and they just don't seem to be working, try imagining sad memories happening to someone else. Or that the sad moment in the scene is happening to someone else. Or imagine these things are happening to someone you care about deeply. Or perhaps they're happening to someone innocent. Then let the tears flow.

**TIP 8:** Bore yourself to tears. This one takes several steps but is quite effective. First close your eyes and mentally get rid of distractions. Then gently rub your eyes for at least 5 seconds. (Be careful if you wear contact lenses.) Next open your eyes and stare at something without blinking. Once you're on the verge of tears recreate a yawn while still not blinking. Viola! Tears.

**TIP 9:** If all else fails and you didn't drink enough water, the air conditioning is drying out your contact lenses, there's no hand sanitizer to be found or you just didn't have time to practice these tips to find the right one for you, there's still one technique left. In real life, we often try to hide our tears. Especially if something happens to you while you're in a public place. This final tip is to be aware of how many people really are looking at you in your current scene. (Unless you're alone. Then be aware of the nearest crew people.) You're being watched and the last thing you want is to break down and cry in front of them. Struggle hard not to show your tears. Hold them in as hard as you can. You will either create a riveting moment as the camera or audience feels your struggle. Or you will actually cry. Either way, you've created a compelling character moment and that is the whole point.

# ABOUT THE AUTHOR

Julie Ann Fay grew up in Lake Charles, Louisiana as the daughter of an elementary school French teacher. Julie fell in love with show business at the age of 5 when she held up a picture of a Christmas tree at a stage performance of Peter Pan. For the next 11 years she studied and performed in many theatrical roles with the Lake Charles Civic Ballet Theatre. After college she put away her dancing shoes but she could not escape the call of the footlights once again when a community theatre production needed backup dancers. From there she has performed in plays such as Auntie Mame , Harvey and My Three Angels. She's acted in 11 short films and 4 feature films and continues to pursue acting and facilitate what she calls "an acting playground for grownups" in Atlanta, Georgia.

CPSIA information can be obtained
at www.ICGtesting.com
Printed in the USA
LVHW051708310121
677942LV00013B/1810